INTENTIONAL PRESBYTERATES

Claiming Our Common Sense of Purpose as Diocesan Priests

— ℰℒ —

ALSO BY
J. RONALD KNOTT

An Encouraging Word
Renewed Hearts, Renewed Church
The Crossroads Publishing Co., 1995

One Heart at a Time
Renewing the Church in the New Millennium
Sophronismos Press, 1999

Sunday Nights
Encouraging Words for Young Adults
Sophronismos Press, 2000

Diocesan Priests in the Archdiocese of Louisville
Archdiocese of Louisville Vocation Office, 2001

Religious Communities in the Archdiocese of Louisville
Archdiocese of Louisville Vocation Office, 2002

For the Record
Encouraging Words for Ordinary Catholics
Sophronismos Press 2003

INTENTIONAL PRESBYTERATES
Claiming Our Common Sense of Purpose
as Diocesan Priests
Sophronismos Press 2003

Copies may be ordered from:

Sophronismos Press
939 Eastern Parkway
Louisville, Kentucky 40217
jrknott@bellsouth.net

INTENTIONAL PRESBYTERATES

Claiming Our Common Sense of Purpose as Diocesan Priests

J. RONALD KNOTT

Sophronismos Press   Louisville, Kentucky

INTENTIONAL PRESBYTERATES
Claiming Our Common Sense of Purpose as Diocesan Priests

Cover design: J. Ronald Knott
Book layout and design: Lori Massey
Cover photo: Bishop McCloskey with the Louisville priests during an 1887 celebration. Photo used by permission of Archi-
vist, Archdiocese of Louisville.

First Printing: November 2003
ISBN 0-9668969-3-9

Printed in the United States of America

Morris Publishing
3212 East Highway 30
Kearney, NE 68847
1-800-650-7888

To our future priests, especially those young men who are responding courageously to the call to diocesan priesthood in today's church.

TABLE OF CONTENTS

PREFACE

"Nothing gets better by leaving it alone."
Winston Churchill

In my twelve years of seminary training, I received a lot of instruction on what a priest is, what a priest needs to know and how to be a priest, but I cannot remember even one hour of training in how to be a member of a presbyterate. Most of us played it by ear.

Even though the new Code of Canon Law says that "(seminary) students are to be so formed that they are prepared for fraternal union with the diocesan presbyterate,"[1] I know of no seminary even today that adequately teaches individual priests-to-be how to be members of their presbyterates. I am not sure they can. It seems to be taken for granted that the newly ordained will pick that up by osmosis or that individual dioceses will tend to that matter. In general, they don't. As a vocation director, I became very concerned about this glaring omission. I have become increasingly alarmed by the fact that our new priests are being inducted into shrinking and demoralized presbyterates to fend for themselves.

There is hope. The National Organization for Continuing Education of Roman Catholic Clergy (NOCERCC) announced on February 3, 2003 the establishment of a fund to provide financial support for a new venture, *Cultivating Unity: the Presbyterate and the Bishop*. The theological foundation for this promising initiative is found in Part III of *The Basic Plan for the Ongoing Formation of Priests*, approved in 2000 by the bishops of the United States. *The Basic Plan* recognizes that priests are "formed" into the common life of a particular presbyterate, making it clear that the vibrancy of each priest's entire life and ministry requires a fundamental ecclesial unity among priests and with their bishop. *Cultivating Unity: the Presbyterate and the Bishop* is NOCERCC's response to this vision and to the bishops' call for leadership in ongoing priestly formation.

We hear a lot about the fact that diocesan priests are not "lone rangers," but the reality of the situation almost insures that we become so by default. On the other hand, neither are we a "good old boys' club." Far from being a fraternity closed in on itself, a truly unified presbyterate dynamically redirects itself outward in pastoral charity and in the gift of themselves to the flock entrusted to them.[2] Neither are presbyterates "religious communities" as such. However, members of the local presbyterate do have a corporate consciousness of being sent. In other words, they "come together" so as to "go out."

When I began to research recent church documents on *presbyterates,* I was shocked to find out how little there actually is on this subject. *The Basic Plan for Ongoing Formation of Priests,* mentioned above, validated my suspicion by saying, "priests are not priests simply one by one, but they are priests and serve the mission of the church in a presbyterate in union with the bishop. The corporate sense of priestly identity and mission, although not fully developed even in official documents, is clearly emerging as an important direction for the future."[3]

There is a lot of material on priesthood, the relationship of individual priests to their bishop and even priests with the laity, but a lack of information on the relationship diocesan priests have with each other in a specific presbyterate, that "intimate sacramental brotherhood" as the Council and the Catechism call it.[4] We have always been warned that we are neither a "religious community" nor a "good old boys' club," but what we actually *are* is waiting to be developed in official church documents.

A few years ago, I started hinting to seminary personnel that it might be a good idea to add such training to the seminary curriculum for diocesan seminarians. One seminary rector heard me and has started promoting this idea to bishops and vocation directors.

In the end, an aggravating parental mantra from my childhood came to mind: "If you want it done right, you have to do it yourself." I may not be "doing it right," but this little book is an attempt to "do it myself." In this small book, I have tried to collect together all that I could from various documents on the subject of presbyterates and to comment on them out of my own personal experience, especially as a vocation director. I hope it will become a help in instructing our seminarians on the basics of being presbyteral members and spark a discussion within my own presbyterate (and maybe other presbyterates as well) about the possibilities for moving from a presbyterate by chance to a presbyterate by intention.

My last book on the diocesan priesthood was entitled *Diocesan Priests in the Archdiocese of Louisville: Partners With the Bishop, Deacons, Consecrated Religious and Lay ministers in the Service of the Church*. If I had to do it over again, I would include another phrase: "partners with each other." This latest effort, *Intentional Presbyterates*, will attempt to address our partnership with each other as a way of reclaiming our common sense of purpose as diocesan priests.

J. Ronald Knott
November, 2003

CHAPTER 1
PRIESTHOOD IN CONTEXT

PRIESTHOOD IN CONTEXT

*Christ gives to priests a particular gift so that they can
help the people of God exercise faithfully and fully
the common priesthood which it has received.*
Pope John Paul II

Since there are a lot of opinions floating around today about what ordained priesthood is, or ought to be, it might be good to summarize what the teaching authority of the church says about ordained ministry before we begin to speak about presbyterates in general.

The following is an attempt to summarize most of the recent church documents on the subject of ordained priesthood in the church: how ordained priests are related to bishops and deacons, how diocesan priests are related to religious order priests, as well as how ordained priests are related to the common priesthood of the laity.[5]

Before Jesus left this earth, he commissioned his followers to carry on his work and to make disciples, baptizing them in the name of the Father, Son and Holy Spirit. So that we might be equipped for this work, he sent the Holy Spirit.

All the baptized, then, are entrusted with the building up of God's people, the church, and the carrying on of some part of Christ's work. There are a variety of specific calls within the general call to carry on Christ's work.

The whole church is a priestly people. Through baptism, all the faithful share in the priesthood of Christ. This participation is called the "common priesthood of the faithful."

Based on this common priesthood and ordered to its service, there exists another participation in the mission of Christ: the ministry conferred by the sacrament of holy orders, where the task is to serve in the name and in the person of Christ in the midst of the community.

Holy Orders is the sacrament through which the mission entrusted by Christ to his apostles continues to be exercised in the church until the end of time: thus it is the sacrament of apostolic ministry.

Ordained ministry differs in essence from the common priesthood of the faithful in that it confers a sacred power for the service of the faithful. Ordained ministers exercise their service to the people of God by preaching the Word, presiding over the sacraments and leading faith communities.

Since the beginning, the ordained ministry has been conferred and exercised in three degrees: that of bishops, priests and deacons. The ministries conferred by ordination are irreplaceable for the organic structure of the church. As St. Ignatius of Antioch wrote, "Without the bishop, presbyters and deacons, one cannot speak of the church."

Priests are united with the bishops in priestly dignity and at the same time depend on them in the exercise of their pastoral functions; they are called to be the bishops' prudent co-workers. They form around their bishop the body of priests that bears responsibility with him for a particular church.

Basically, there are two ways to serve the church as a priest: either as a "diocesan" priest or a "religious order" priest. "When the call to the priesthood is coupled with an attraction to being with the people of God in a given place, the local church or diocese, and serving them particularly in parish ministry, then the call points to diocesan priesthood."[6] "Not only are (diocesan priests) called forth from the laity to be priests, but they choose to continue to live among lay people, to lead communities of lay men and women, and to focus their ministry on the mission and spirituality of the laity."[7] All priests are sent forth as co-workers in the same undertaking, whether they are engaged in a parochial or supra-parochial ministry, whether they dedicate their efforts to scientific research or teaching, whether by manual labor they share in the lot of the workers themselves ... or whether they fulfill any other apostolic tasks or labors related to the apostolate.[8]

A diocesan priest usually serves his whole life in the boundaries of one particular geographical area, known as a diocese, under the leadership of a local bishop, to whom he makes promises of celibacy and obedience. Usually a diocesan priest is called to specialize in parish ministry or other diocesan service.

A religious order priest takes vows, serves, lives and prays in community with and follows the rule of the order of which he is a member. Some religious order priests work in parishes like diocesan priests. While diocesan priests usually work within one diocese throughout their lives, religious order priests may be sent to other states or even other countries to work wherever their community needs them. While working in a particular diocese, religious order priests make up part of that local presbyterate.[9]

CHAPTER 2
WHAT IS A
PRESBYTERATE?

———— ঞ ————

WHAT IS A PRESBYTERATE?

It is a terrible thing to look over your shoulder when you are trying
to lead – and find no one there.
Franklin D. Roosevelt

F rom the scarcity of material on presbyterates in recent
church documents, the most significant definition is a
small paragraph from "The Decree on the Ministry and
Life of Priests" from Vatican Council II. All else seems to be
commentary.

> ... all priests are united among themselves in an
> intimate sacramental brotherhood. In a special
> way they form one presbytery in a diocese to
> whose service they are committed under their
> own bishop. For even though priests are assigned
> to different duties they still carry on one priestly
> ministry on behalf of men.[10]

The careful wording of this decree keeps the distinction of
a worldwide presbyterate through which all priests relate to the
worldwide episcopate and the local brotherhood of priests to
their bishop in a particular diocese. The *college of bishops* is of
divine ordinance; the diocesan *presbyterium* is of ecclesiastical
law. These bodies of priests cannot be considered apart from
their bishops. Their *raison d'être* is to be together with, and
under, the bishop.[11]

This sacramental brotherhood at the level of the local church
implies that each member is bound to the others through a
sense of common purpose and a spirit of collaboration in diocesan mission.[12] The Sacrament of Holy Orders is conferred
upon each of them as individuals, but they are inserted into

the communion of the presbyterate united with the Bishop.[13] "... Priests are not priests simply one by one, but they are priests and serve the mission of the church in a presbyterate with the bishop."[14] "... The priest is called in particular to grow ... in and with his own presbyterate in union with his bishop."[15] "... No priest can in isolation or single-handedly accomplish his mission in a satisfactory way. He can do so only by joining forces under the direction of church authorities. Each and every priest, therefore, is joined to his brother priests by a bond of charity, prayer and every kind of cooperation."[16]

"The ongoing formation of a presbyterate (as distinct from an individual priest's ongoing formation) is the deliberate cultivation of the unity of the priests and their bishop ..."[17] "It is clear that the ongoing formation of presbyterates is significant for the vitality of the church's mission. It is also clear that the formation of presbyterates centers on cultivating unity."[18] The formation of a presbyterate in its unity and fraternity aims, ultimately, (a) to promote a more intense pastoral effectiveness and (b) to be a sacramental sign for the world to be drawn to the very life of the Trinity. Jesus prays for unity among his disciples, especially those who will have the apostolic mission.[19] Flowing from this reality of presbytery is a spirit of service or ministry among priests to each other – bridging differences that rise out of a variety of experiences, appreciative of the perspectives and gifts of religious and diocesan clergy, being a "concerned other" for priests in need, supporting spiritual activities by presence and participation, being active in priests' associations.[20]

"... It can be useful to eliminate what presbyteral unity is *not*. Presbyteral unity, for example, is obviously not based on blood relationships. Nor is it dependent on friendship or even like-mindedness. It does not mean that everyone must be the same. And, of course, presbyteral unity is never legitimately anchored into an attitude of superiority or chauvinism, which is in fact clericalism."[21] Priests who form a presbyterate are called from the laity, live among the laity, so as to empower the laity. With a "corporate consciousness of being sent," they come together so as to go out.

The ministry of priests is not confined to the care of the faithful as individuals, but is also extended to the formation of a genuine Christian community. Priests are, in the name of the bishop, defenders of the common good. It is their task to reconcile differences of mentality in such a way that no one feels a stranger in the community of the faithful. "No one can give what he does not possess." If we are going to be the formers of community, then we need to know how to be members of one, namely, our own "intimate sacramental brotherhood," our own presbyterate.

CHAPTER 3
WHY DO WE NEED INTENTIONAL PRESBYTERATES?

—————— ɞ ——————

WHY DO WE NEED INTENTIONAL PRESBYTERATES?

He that will not apply new remedies must expect new evils.
Francis Bacon

66 **I**n spite of the unprecedented challenges and ordeals engulfing the priesthood at the turn of the millennium, the *esprit de corps* long associated with Catholic clergy refuses to buckle. The fraternity holds. As the millennium's first rays of dawn catch the contours of the changing face of priesthood, priests still sense they are members of a mysterious brotherhood that continues to shape their lives and world view. Not only is their pastoral identity grounded in the covenant of ordination, they experience a spiritual bond linking them to priests the world over, indeed priests from ages past and to the priests of ages yet to come."[22]

Even though many of these sentiments may still be true, it might be important to note that these words were written immediately before the recent "sexual abuse scandal" that has engulfed American presbyterates. While there are many good things going on in today's presbyterates, and many of them have long and proud traditions, taking past successes for granted is lethal in today's church. The glue that has held us together in the past is breaking down. Today, more than ever, we must be intentional about our "groupness." "The bond of unity within the presbyterate really needs to be stronger today than ever before …"[23] What we are looking for is a corporate consciousness, a mission in companionship that will fire and unite not only the presbyterate itself, but also the whole diocesan church.[24]

The Basic Plan for the Ongoing Formation of Priests ends with an observation that I came to on my own. "The corporate sense of priestly identity and mission, although not fully developed in official documents, is clearly emerging as an important direction for the future."[25] A "corporate sense of priestly identity and mission" may not yet be "fully developed," but the need for such a corporate sense is now. A presbyterate with a "corporate sense of priestly identity and mission" does not happen automatically. It must be intentional. Intentional presbyterates must be willed into existence by those individual members who are concerned enough to make the commitment to see that it happens.

(1) Why now? To say that presbyterates across the country are facing a dilemma these days is so much an understatement that it is almost laughable. "Dilemma" is the perfect word for our situation, because "dilemma" means "two horns," one horn being "crisis" and the other horn being "opportunity." Obviously, we have a crisis, but maybe not as obvious is the opportunity we have. Gregg Levoy, in his book *Callings,* writes, "An ordeal may serve the purpose of shaking us loose from our moorings in order to set us up for important changes we can't see or imagine yet."[26]

(2) "An Army of One" may be the U.S. Army's motto, but it could be ours as well. In the ordination rite the priests present each impose hands on the candidate and then gather around the bishop as he prays the principal consecratory prayer. By doing that, we participate in welcoming and celebrate the arrival of a new member into our "intimate sacramental brotherhood." "The rite of the imposition of hands by the bishop and all the priests ... has special significance and merit because it points ... to the fact that the priest cannot act by himself; he acts within the presbyterate becoming a brother of all those who constitute it."[27]

"Yet the reality is that sometimes members of presbyterates are set against one another. They are a house divided rather than a family gathered. Some presbyterates are divided ideologically, camps that vie against one another. Diocesan priests find themselves competing against one another, reluctant to applaud anyone else's work for fear it will take away from theirs. Some priests would rather do anything than join brother priests for prayer or for learning or just for fun."[28] This has never been acceptable and, especially now, it can be lethal to presbyterates.

(3) One of the stated reasons for intentional presbyterates is that it promises a more intense pastoral effectiveness. With our numbers shrinking and our responsibilities growing, when have we needed to work as a team more than now? Since we cannot work much harder, we must work smarter, and the smartest way to work is to be intentional about working as a team. Why should we be surprised that parishes cannot work together, when we priests cannot?

(4) Priest shortage! Priest shortage! All the statistics tell us that healthy contact with priests is the reason most young adults make the move toward answering their call to ordained priesthood. One happy and effective priest can do more to promote vocations to diocesan priesthood than a hundred eye-catching billboards. A team of happy and effective priests can do more to promote vocations to diocesan priesthood than a million dollars' worth of clever TV spots. One of my favorite passages on vocations from Vatican II is this one: "Let him (priest) attract the hearts of young people to the priesthood by his own humble and energetic life, joyfully pursued, and **by love for his fellow priests and brotherly collaboration with them**."[29] Our best chance for attracting vocations to our way of life is to become more "attractive" individually **and** as a group. How do we become "attractive?" We become more attractive by being what we say we are: partners with the bishop with a corporate consciousness of being sent, with energetic lives joyfully pursued.

(5) I guess the first time I started thinking about the need for intentional presbyterates was shortly after I was ordained. My first assignment was to work in our "home missions." I was sent as far away from other priests as I could be sent in our diocese. Within five years I was living and working alone in two

counties. After a few years down there, I was attending a gathering of priests when one of my fellow priests asked me, after I had introduced myself, "What diocese are you in, Father?" I remember answering, quite irritated, "Yours, Father!"

Today, with more than 25% of our new priests being foreign born, some without families, and many others coming to us as new Catholics through the RCIA process, we must be more intentional than ever about how we welcome and mentor new members, not just into the priesthood, but into our presbyterates. This calls not just for normal one-on-one mentoring, but for group mentoring. In the "old days" we came into our presbyterate in groups of 10-12 after attending seminary together, often for 12 years. Many are coming to us today one at a time after five years or less of seminary training. Our old ways are no longer adequate. We ignore this new reality to our peril and theirs. I have been asked more than once by seminarians, "Will I be alone?" I usually lie a little, but if I told the truth, the answer would be, in most cases, "Yes, unless you solve the problem for yourself."

(6) St. Paul wrote these words to his fellow missionary, Timothy: "Fan into flame the gift God gave you when I laid hands on you." (I Tim. 1:6) We, priests and presbyterates, are daily bombarded with new information. If we are to incorporate this new information, we must continually revise our maps of reality, and sometimes when enough new information has accumulated we must make major revisions. This process of making revisions, particularly major revisions, is painful, sometimes excruciatingly painful. What happens when we have striven long and hard to develop a working view of the world, a seemingly workable map, and then we are confronted with new information suggesting that the map needs to be redrawn? The painful effort required seems frightening, almost overwhelming. What we do, more often than not, is to ignore the new information. Sadly, when we do that, we expend more energy in defending an outmoded view of the world than would have been required to revise and correct it in the first place.[30]

There is always a part of us that does not want to exert ourselves, that clings to the old and familiar, fearful of any change or effort, desiring comfort at any cost and absence of pain at any price, even if the penalty is ineffectiveness and stagnation.[31]

As presbyterates, we are being called to re-form ourselves by incorporating the new realities that are staring us in the face. For our own sakes, for the sake of the mission we have been given and for the sake of future new members, we are being called as presbyterates to regroup, to recommit and to "fan into flame the gift that God gave us."

(7) There are serious dangers in leaving presbyterates to chance. I find it frightening to observe in other priests and feel within myself that pull to isolate oneself from the chaos of today's presbyterates. One priest called this isolation "going into private practice." We are called by the church to make every effort to avoid living our priesthood in an isolated and subjective way and try to enhance fraternal communion in giving and receiving – from priest to priest – of the warmth of friendship, of affectionate help, of acceptance and fraternal correction.[32]

Sadly, the usual practice is to ordain individuals and then set them loose on the people, without support and accountability, to do ministry however they choose to define it. These "lone rangers" often put themselves and the laity at risk by their destructive and uninformed actions. This is especially true for the youngest. Because ordination is often considered a final state, where nothing more **has** to be done, his elevation to priesthood is likely to freeze him, if isolated, at his adolescent level of adjustment.[33]

Intentional presbyterates may be our best insurance for keeping the vocations we have. Recent research, led by Dean R. Hoge at Catholic University, found that 10 to 15 percent of priests resigned in the first five years of ministry due to loneliness, feelings of being unappreciated, problems of celibacy and disillusionment.[34]

(8) Without intentional presbyterates, some young priests have latched onto the trappings and forms of priesthood from bygone days for their sense of purpose and security. Instead of creating a new way to be an intimate sacramental brotherhood, one that embraces and promotes the ministry of the laity, they settle for dressing up and trying to reenact some imagined "good old days" when priests knew who they were, lay people stayed in their places and all things were right in the heavens. Equally missing the target are those who are out there "doing their own thing," living a priesthood of "private practice," doing ministry however they choose to define it. Most pathetic of all are those who have dropped out psychologically, merely going through the motions of priesthood.

Those who look back may be looking for the right thing, but looking for it in all the wrong places, just as those who are "doing their own thing" are doing. Both ask too little. What is needed in the priesthood is not a restoration, certainly not more disintegration, but a transformation. Restoration is about trying to return to the past. The disintegration of the present is scary, but even some of it can be good, if it leads to new life and not just more death. Transformation is about the future, about "making old things new." Restoration is about things changing. Transformation is about people changing. Only a "group change of heart" will lead to a true renewal of our presbyterates.

(9) I have heard so much about the predictions of how few priests we will have in 2010 and how we will stretch them to fit our parishes, but nobody seems to be asking my question: "Just what condition do you think these remaining priests will be in when 2010 rolls around?" I am firmly convinced that we will not "get better" by leaving things alone, but through a deliberate and decisive will to do so. I don't think it is inevitable that we degenerate into a small band of old Shakers, but I do believe intentional presbyterates are possible – if we do act decisively, now! It was my dream as a vocation director to collaborate with my fellow priests so as to "fan into flame" the energy and joy we so desperately need to have and project. It is a "must" if more young men are going to be attracted to our

way of life. If we don't do this for each other, then we will all be left to take care of ourselves, one "lone ranger" at a time.

(10) Presbyterates today have been described as a "house divided." If presbyteral unity is the goal, then we must intentionally and accurately identify and honestly confront the divisions that impede and imperil our unity. As Abraham Lincoln said, "A house divided against itself cannot stand." There are serious consequences to be faced if these divisions are ignored or left to fester. Once named, they can be addressed. Addressing them prepares the way for a more constructive approach to presbyteral formation.

- **Competition.** Priests, like other men ministering in an American cultural context, find themselves socialized by a pattern of competition and comparison evident in contemporary American culture. This competition and comparison can easily foster division.

- **Different Generations in a Presbyterate.** A single presbyterate can easily contain at least four different "formational generations": (1) pre-Vatican II, (2) pre- and post-Vatican II, (3) post-Vatican II and (4) a new emergent formational generation. Priests from these generations must work side by side, but often they do so uneasily and sometimes with apparent divisions.

- **Clerical Envy.** Clerical envy has always been with us (cf. John 21:20-22). In a hierarchical structure (which parallels business, the military, or government/politics), one might assume that advancement would be correlative to higher rank, greater responsibility or a bigger paycheck. This is not so in the priesthood. Progress in priestly ministry is measured solely on being a better sacramental sign and doing better the tasks of priestly ministry. When there is a lack of clarity about advancement or its symbols, priests will respond to what they *think* is the presence of such signs in others and the lack in themselves. This is fertile ground for breeding divisions.

- **Lack of Attention from the Bishop**. Bishops have many responsibilities. Even though presbyteral unity is ultimately their responsibility, in reality it can slip to a lower end of a long list of priorities. This neglect favors divisions and, ultimately, spawns a number of problems in a diocese.

- **Varied Backgrounds**. Priests in the past followed a predictable pattern. Candidates now come into the seminary at different points and with varying life and work experiences. Although diversity can be enriching, it makes unity and cohesiveness in the presbyterate more challenging and, in fact, can lead to divisions.

- **Varied Theologies and Spiritualities**. Although our faith is one, it can take a number of expressions in theological forms. The current state of theological pluralism can fracture the ability of priests to talk to each other in a common theological language. Likewise, differences in spiritualities (the practice of the faith) can impede a sense of unity and lead to divisions.

- **Varied Languages, Cultures and Places of Origin**. We have never ceased to be an immigrant country, and this fact has had (and continues to have) an impact on the church. Priests come into presbyterates with different racial, cultural and language backgrounds. Although these differences can be enriching, frequently they create dividing lines and cause divisions.

These divisions have significant consequences. They lead to diminished effectiveness that undermines the utilization of valuable human resources needed to address pressing issues. When these divisions are public, and they usually are, they constitute an anti-sign for the community and discourage those who might feel called to the priesthood. Finally, divisions can shift the focus of priests from a wide-ranging diocesan perspective to an anti-Catholic, narrow, localized emphasis on one's own parish with a resultant parochialism or congregationalism.[35]

(11) If women and married men continue to be excluded from priesthood and the quality of lay ministry continues to intensify, the least we can do as a body of priests is to get our act together to serve them well and to work with them as partners in ministry. My sense is that lay people are sick to death of the immaturity, bad service, incompetence and inability to lead coming from some priests. Lay people today expect, and deserve, competent pastors with the ability to elicit from and coordinate the charisms of lay people.

Without a close connection to a presbyterate, priests are left to define ministry however they choose to define it, putting themselves and the laity at risk. This can lead to two extremes: (a) authoritarianism and (b) abdication.

Authoritarianism dismisses the rightful role of others as also responsible for carrying on some part of Christ's work, given to them at baptism. Priests today must remember that when authority is **duly** exercised, it is done not so much to command as to serve. True power derives from the ability to make other people powerful. In those areas where he is obliged to exercise it, exercising **proper** authority is a gift to the church.

Abdication of responsibility is equally destructive to the church. Many priests have assumed that encouraging lay ministry means the abdication of their pastoral authority, allowing all manner of craziness to fill the vacuum.

"Those in authority must overcome the temptation to exempt themselves from this responsibility. If they do not exercise this authority, they no longer serve. In close communion with his Bishop and his faithful, the priest should avoid introducing into his pastoral ministry all forms of authoritarianism and forms of democratic administration that are alien to the profound reality of the ministry, for these lead to a secularization of the priest and a clericalization of the laity. Behind such approaches to the ministry there is often a hidden fear of assuming responsibility or naming mistakes, of not being liked or of being unpopular, or, indeed, reluctance to accept the cross."[36]

Priests are called not only to be leaders of the community, but also teachers of the Word and ministers of the sacraments. Many priests have discovered, as well, that the handing over of administrative duties to others does not mean that all of a sudden they are left with extraordinary **spiritual** leadership skills. It's a lot easier to balance a budget than inspire a congregation to move into a new level of discipleship. As spiritual directors of the community, we must strive not only to be good ourselves, but also to be good at what we do, being good "group spiritual directors" of the congregations entrusted to us.

(12) We need intentional presbyterates, especially now, **precisely because**, as a group, we are tired. *Reflections on the Morale of Priests,* a 1988 document of the NCCB Committee on Priestly Life and Ministry, made this sad observation: "Among some priests, there is a significant number who have settled for a part-time presence to their priesthood. ... They elect to drop out quietly. Many more of our priests believed in renewal, were willing to adapt, worked hard and are now just plain tired."[37]

"I Will Give You Shepherds" warns young priests about the dangers of being tired. "With priests who have just come out of the seminary, a certain sense of "having had enough" is quite understandable when faced with new times for study and meeting. But the idea that priestly formation ends on the day one leaves the seminary is false and dangerous, and needs to be totally rejected."[38]

(13) Finally, assuming we will continue receiving new members into our presbyterates, we need intentional presbyterates for the sake of those who will follow us. The "millennial generation," young adults entering college beginning in 2000, has been characterized as "used to structure," "trusting organizations and authority," "more collegial by experience" and "liking to work together in teams to complete and resolve problems." They assert that the predominant cause of the problems in our culture is "selfishness."[39] A "lone-ranger" approach to priesthood will not be attractive to this generation. What will be attractive to this new generation of priests will be the "com-

munion with" and the "common sense of purpose" of presbyterates.

I once heard a story about St. Bernard and his monks, who traveled through France on foot. They were so happy and attractive that, when they passed through some towns, parents hid their children out of fear that they would run off and join them. Today some parents hide their children out of fear they will be unhappy if they do join us.

CHAPTER 4
WHOSE JOB IS IT TO FORM INTENTIONAL PRESBYTERATES?

———— හ ————

WHOSE JOB IS IT TO FORM INTENTIONAL PRESBYTERATES?

There go my people. I must find out where they are going so that I can lead them.
Alexandre Ledru-Rollin, French politician

There is an old story from childhood that I remember well. "Who Will Bell the Cat" is a story about several mice meeting inside a wall. Outside, in the room, lies a multitude of cheese, sausage and other food. Unfortunately, patrolling around the food is a large, hungry cat. After brainstorming the situation, the mice came to the conclusion that the best way to approach the situation was to fasten a bell to the cat's neck so that they could grab the food and escape when they heard the bell on the approaching cat. They were so excited about their plan until someone asked, "And who, my dear mice, will place the bell around the cat's neck?" With that, they all fell silent. The point of the story is simple: good ideas mean nothing unless someone is willing to implement them.

In theory, it is the bishop's responsibility to see to the spiritual, intellectual, and material condition of his priests so that they can live holy and pious lives and fulfill their ministry faithfully and fruitfully.[40] As quoted previously, in reality, "A bishop has many responsibilities, and many things claim his attention. Presbyteral unity may not seem to be as pressing, for example, as dealing with individual priests who are problematic, with the distribution and assignment of clergy, or with the recruitment of new candidates. Working for presbyteral unity can slip to a lower end of a list of priorities. In fact, its neglect favors divisions and ultimately, a number of attendant problems in a diocese."[41]

So who will "bell the cat" when it comes to creating "intentional presbyterates?" Even though it is ideally the bishop's role to build cohesive and effective presbyterates, in reality this leadership must be shared from within the presbyterate itself. Whoever the priest-leaders are, an intentional presbyterate cannot be unleashed by priests who have no personal passion for it, nor by priests with the inability to visualize it, nor by priests who simply wish it would happen – but rather by priests who can imagine it, priests who have a burning desire to see it happen and priests who have the ability to marshal the troops to make it happen. The commitment and clarity of these leaders can unleash the power of the team, and the power of the team directs individual accomplishments toward organizational goals. Leaders look into the future and see the organization not as it is, but as it could be.

Among those leaders helping the bishop with his responsibility of presbyteral formation and unity are the Priests' Council, the director of ongoing formation, the vocation director, the health panel, and those who deal with the needs of senior priests (who, by the way, have a special role of recalling and reminding the presbyterate of their collective history and sense of mission).

Finally, no presbyterate can be led to intentionality unless individual members of that presbyterate are willing to be led. If the leaders are credible, those who are willing to be part of this coalition will recognize their voices and follow their lead in unleashing the potential power of the team. As the Book of Proverbs (29:18) says, "Without a vision, the people perish." Without a vision, presbyterates perish as well.

CHAPTER 5
CREATING A PLAN
AND PUTTING IT
INTO ACTION

———— ℰℴ ————

CREATING A PLAN AND PUTTING IT INTO ACTION

*The crisis consists precisely in the fact that the old is dying
and the new cannot be born. In this interregnum, a great
variety of morbid symptoms appear.*
Antonio Gramsci, political activist

I It is one thing to diagnose a problem; it is another to know what to do to resolve it. Even if we do **want** an intentional presbyterate and even if we have **leaders** willing to work toward that dream, **how to do it** is still left for consideration. Here I am reminded of an old story I read years ago.

A certain weasel, long afflicted with neurotic symptoms, was accustomed to regular consultation with his psychiatrist, a wise old owl. As therapy progressed, the weasel, becoming disaffected with the long probing, the attempt to achieve insight into unconscious motivation and the wearisome effort to release emotional tensions, demanded of the owl, "Tell me what I should **do**!"

Taken aback both by the unexpected nature and by the vehemence of the demand, the owl abandoned his customary reserve and ventured direct advice. "I think, my dear weasel," he said at last, "that the only solution to your problem is to turn yourself into a frog."

The weasel was astonished at this advice and replied, "Thank you for your advice, which I fully tend to heed. One problem remains, however. I pray, sir, tell me how I go about turning myself into a frog."

To this the owl replied, with a certain measure of disdain, "My dear weasel, please be kind enough not to bother me with these operational problems."[42]

1. A Priestly Life and Ministry Cluster

If we are to have intentional presbyterates, the place to begin, it would seem to me, is to look at how we are organized now. In many dioceses, including my own, there are several offices that deal with the ministry and lives of priests, but they do not formally collaborate. While most offices are doing a decent job, there is no regular dialogue among them. It seems to me that if the goal is to have a unified presbyterate, the place to begin would be to create some kind of "priestly life and ministry cluster" so the left hand will know what the right hand is doing. Regular collaboration should take place among the vocation office, the priest personnel office, the continuing education office, the priests' health panel and the office of retired priests. This cluster, coming together for regular collaboration, could help focus our common wisdom toward strengthening us individually and as a group.

The first goal of such a cluster would be to look at everything that is already available to support priests (as a group and individually), to identify what is missing, and to put it all back together in a comprehensive and intentional plan for ongoing presbyteral health and effectiveness.

2. What help is currently available?

Many priests under-use, or may even be ignorant of, the help that is already available to them. Most dioceses have all or some of the following supports.

- The laity
- The bishop
- Fellow priests
- Family and friends
- Financial compensation
- Office of clergy personnel

- Continuing formation of the clergy office
- Clergy health panel
- Priests' council
- Vicar for clergy
- Retired housing
- Presbyteral assembly
- Support groups
- Annual retreats, prayer days and prayer groups
- Sabbaticals
- Spiritual directors
- Alternative housing
- Vacations
- Chrism Mass
- Clergy Day
- Priests' Jubilee celebration
- Ordination celebrations

3. Doing Group Maintenance: The Role of the Presbyteral Assembly

A "priestly life and ministry cluster" could be the nucleus of a team created to refocus attention on the continued health and effectiveness not only of individual members of a presbyterate, but also of the presbyterate as a team. For continued health and effectiveness, every organization needs to tend to "task maintenance" (getting the job done well) and "group maintenance" (taking good care of those who do the job). "Task maintenance" tends to the *effectiveness* of those who do ministry. "Group maintenance" tends to the *health and cohesiveness* of those who do ministry. Continuing education offices deal primarily with the *effectiveness* of ministry. Groups like the health panel take care of **individual priests** who do the ministry. The premier event that deals with the health and cohesiveness of the **group**, the event that could focus most effectively on forming intentional presbyterates, I believe, is the annual Presbyteral Assembly. For this reason, the planning of this annual assembly should be a major concern of the "priestly life and ministry cluster" since they have, together, the big picture of what is going on in our presbyterates.

An important part of doing "group maintenance" is mentoring new members into the presbyterate. This will necessitate the need to include seminarians in as many presbyteral functions as possible (and to schedule them so that they can). Seminarians need to know not only how to be a good seminarian, but also how to be a good priest. Even though some would like to look at the recruitment and training of seminarians as separate from the issues facing presbyterates, I do not share that view. I fought against this "not in front of the kids" mentality throughout my time as a vocation director. Some believe that since seminarians are not yet priests, they should be treated as something radically different until after their ordinations. I do not accept this view any more than I accept the view that a fetus is not a baby until it is actually born or that prenatal care has nothing to do with the later health of that child. Even wolves wait **together** at the lair for the birth of a cub and, once born, the whole pack takes responsibility for, and participates in, training them to work as a team and to be contributing members of their pack.

As Pope John Paul II said in "I Will Give You Shepherds," the bishop can rely above all on the cooperation of his presbyterate (in promoting vocations). **All** its priests are united to the bishop and share his responsibility in seeking **and** fostering vocations."[43]

The facts are that more than 25% of all new priests now are "foreign born," and many others are "converts." As a group, their seminary training has been dramatically shortened compared with that of priests in the past. While these "outsiders" have the chance of working with three or four pastors during summer assignments, it is usually not possible for them to meet most of the presbyterate until after their ordinations. It is simply too dangerous to continue this practice of introducing new priests to their presbyterates on their ordination days and putting the burden on them to find their own way in bonding with the group. Paul de Becker, in a recent article in *The Tablet* titled "A Priest Alone," says of the newly ordained who struggle in ministry: "A root cause of their unhappiness and a major element in their lives is an intense loneliness."[44]

It is insane to warn a new priest not to become a "lone ranger" and then not give him an alternative. As Bishop Gerald Kicanas, a former seminary rector and now a bishop, has said, "The call to priesthood would be responded to more freely if the fear of intense loneliness were not as prominent."[45]

Including and involving seminarians in presbyteral assemblies, from the beginning, gives them a chance to get to know most priests before ordination. Such an involvement gives most priests an opportunity to support those in training and tell them how much we value their sacrifices, even if their parish has no seminarians or has not had the chance to welcome one of them for a summer placement. Priests-to-be need to see us and hear from us, and we need to see them and hear from them as well. All the recent research tells us that contact with priests is still the best way to promote and keep vocations to the priesthood. When that is not done, most other efforts fail.

A lot has been said about making attendance at presbyteral assemblies "mandatory." While I believe that the bishop has the right to demand participation for the sake of the group, I believe the better path is for those who plan these assemblies to make them so attractive that most will **want** to attend. Force is useless. Let it be a coalition of the "willing," not of the "coerced."

4. A "Pastors in Training" Program

Besides the "group mentoring into the presbyterate by the whole presbyterate" that should begin as soon as a seminarian is accepted by the diocese (see section 3), there is a serious need for individual mentors for the newly ordained, leading up to and including a first pastorate.

Problem: In recent years, the newly ordained and new pastors have been assigned a priest mentor, usually a model pastor. The results have been mixed. One of the main problems being reported is the failure to meet regularly. A fine pastor may not have the time necessary for this work. A model pastor may not know how to teach what he knows.

Possible Solution: Choose a small group of our best re-tired priests, maybe three who are willing to serve as "group mentors" for new pastors. Do some initial formation and train-ing of that group, and choose a leader.

Problem: The newly ordained are being named pastors in a year or two. Seminary did not and cannot prepare them to be pastors. Associate pastors are reporting that they are nei-ther fish nor fowl, with no real position in many parish struc-tures. A week-long or weekend orientation for being a pastor is not adequate.

Solution: Once a new priest is ordained, he could be called a "pastor in formation" while serving as an "associate pastor" at a designated parish. Because no single small diocese would have enough "new pastors" for their own program, a new in-ter-diocesan "pastors in formation" program could be mapped out by the continuing education directors of neighboring dio-ceses. Because it is "inter-diocesan," various types of groups could formed around the various types of parishes they will be going into: urban parishes, rural parishes, home mission par-ishes, clustered parishes, ethnic parishes. A qualified leader for the group should be selected and trained, if necessary. Be-cause of all its resources, this leader and this group of new pastors-to-be could hold their quarterly meetings at the "re-gional center for sustaining pastoral excellence" (see section 5). Problems and situations are presented and worked through by the group. Exceptional pastors, lay ministry leaders and other professionals would be asked to be presenters in this program. Anyone who hopes to become a pastor should meet the basic requirements of this program. An evaluation of their participation and learning is presented to the bishop and per-sonnel committee for consideration in an assignment as pas-tor.

Problem: Many times entry-into-new-pastorate-problems are not addressed as they happen, but are left to fester. Often only the priest is asked about how things are going. Asking the new pastor to self-report his problems is an unreal expec-tation.

Solution: Once the new pastor has been named, the group mentors should meet with his parish council before he begins; with the new pastor, his staff and parish council six months into the process; and again six months after that until it has been established that it is no longer necessary. Regular reports are made to the bishop until he is no longer considered a "new pastor."

5. Regional Centers For Sustaining Pastoral Excellence

Seminary is not enough! I learned that as soon as I was ordained. Like all my classmates, I was trained to be an associate pastor in a large suburban parish or small city parish. I was expected to learn to be a pastor on the job over a ten- to twelve-year period. However, I was sent to our "home missions." It was unusual in 1975, but I ended up being a pastor after five years. I was not prepared to start a new parish, to live alone or to understand the dynamics of the "bible belt." I had to learn on the job. Cut off from most other priests, I had to teach myself. Neither was I prepared to handle the rural parish and an old cathedral in need of revitalization that followed my first assignment. I was left to figure out what to do on my own.

In 2003, we are still ordaining good men and sending them into ministry situations that they are not prepared to handle, with shallow and haphazard support systems and disconnected ongoing education programs. When these young pastors crash and burn, we seem surprised and, in many cases, blame the victim or the seminary that trained them. This is exacerbated by the fact that young priests are now being given large parishes within a year or two after ordination, and many of those young priests are foreign born or recent "converts."

Most American seminaries are doing a heroic job at what they do, but there is no way they can accomplish everything that is needed while these young men are in the seminary. All that seminaries can realistically offer, under their present configuration, is a sound theological base and a taste of pastoral ministry. They cannot do all that is necessary to prepare serious pastoral leaders before ordination.

What we need, I believe, are "regional centers for sustaining pastoral excellence" designed to support priests **in** ministry. These regional centers should be just as serious in their approach as our seminaries are at preparing priests to **enter** ministry. Since Vatican II, we have put all our eggs in the workshop-convention model of continuing education. That model is increasingly inadequate. What we need is something organized, intentional, structured, lifelong and, in some cases, mandatory. This kind of program must be focused not so much on academics, but on helping priests to do their work well by staying healthy, engaged and prepared to meet the new challenges they face, whether they be in a first pastorate or a rural, missionary, inner-city or multicultural parish or ministry situation.

This kind of serious, well-thought-out approach to the practice of ministry needs, in most cases, to be accomplished across diocesan lines. Very few dioceses have the resources and skilled personnel to adequately teach these skills. A serious collaboration among the continuing formation directors of neighboring dioceses could lead to the foundation of such an enterprise. As far as money, most priests do not use the continuing education funds already available to them.

With some renovation and expansion, already existing seminary sites would be ideal. They already have theological libraries, bookstores, spiritual directors, confessors, chapels, liturgies, housing, an established communication network, gyms and retreat-like atmospheres. These "regional centers for sustaining pastoral excellence," sharing the same campus with seminarians, could complete a seminary's mission of providing well-trained diocesan priests for its client dioceses. Having these centers on the campus of, but separate from, the seminary could raise the theological level of priests, while providing an on-site laboratory for seminarians to observe real pastoral ministers in dialogue and problem solving. Add ongoing deacon and lay ministry formation, and the picture is even more complete.

As a vocation director, I was not only interested in attracting more vocations to priesthood, but also in keeping the vocations we have happy, healthy and effective. In that job, I tried to train our seminarians to "mind their calls" after ordination, but I am only one person. All priests share in the duty. We need to give each other that challenge, but we also need to give each other the structures to do it.

CHAPTER 6
A SAMPLE
PRESBYTERAL
ASSEMBLY

— ༄ —

A SAMPLE PRESBYTERAL ASSEMBLY

"The leavers have adjusted better than the stayers."
Exxon VP, describing the aftermath of the company's down-sizing

FAN INTO FLAME

A PRESBYTERAL ASSEMBLY ON BECOMING "AN INTENTIONAL PRESBYTERATE"

"Fan into flame the gift God gave you
when I laid hands on you."
I Timothy 1:6

GOALS:

A. TO MOVE TO A CONSENSUS ON A NEW VISION FOR OUR PRESBYTERATE BUILT ON THE OLD,

B. TO INVITE THE GROUP TO COMMIT TO THAT NEW VISION, AND

C. TO FIND WAYS TO KEEP THAT NEW VISION BEFORE OUR EYES AND TO PASS IT ON TO NEW MEMBERS.

INPUT SECTION

I. THE VISION

A Preaching Event Based on I Timothy 1:6-14 "Fanning the Flame and Rekindling the Fire"

The Charism of a Diocesan Priest: What Is Our Common Purpose, and What Makes Us Different?

Presbyterates are not religious communities, but what are they? What does the church say about presbyterates? (An overview of the documents)

The speaker will review and condense the church documents that deal with "the presbyterate." The resulting document will become part of an orientation manual for present members of the presbyterate as well as an orientation for new members coming in.

Our Presbyterate: A Historical Overview

The speaker will be encouraged to write a short history of the local presbyterate tracing the forces that have played a part of who it is, including the absorption of immigrants, previous scandals and shortages. This, too will become part of the orientation manual for presbyterate members.

Our Presbyterate: Experiences and Dreams

A. **Our Past: What was lost, what was found?** An older priest's reflection on the presbyterate he has known. It is expected that he will interview other older priests as part of that reflection.

B. **Our Future: Hopes and Fears.** The speaker here will summarize the hopes and fears of the young members of the local presbyterate. Again, it is expected that the speaker will summarize his conversations with other newly ordained and older seminarians.

PROCESS SECTION

II. WRITING A NEW VISION

What are our individual responsibilities to the presbyterate?

What are the responsibilities of the presbyterate to us as individuals?

What help is available to us as members of the presbyterate? What help is needed? A review and new goals

The "Priestly Life and Ministry Cluster" and a new mission statement for the presbyteral assembly

A review of annual presbyteral celebrations: What works and what doesn't? What would work better?

INPUT SECTION

III. OVERCOMING OBSTACLES

Clashing Ecclesiologies: Moving from a Point of View to a Viewing Point

Great Expectations:

A. What the laity need from their priests: A panel of lay ministers

B. What the bishop needs from his priests

C. What priests need from the laity and their bishop

How Do we Get More Members to Participate? A report from a task force on why some priests do not attend

What is it Like to Enter our Presbyterate as an Outsider?

A. Input from a newly incardinated priest

B. Input from foreign-born seminarians and priests

CELEBRATION SECTION

IV. COMMITTING TO THE VISION

Bishop's talk

Closing Eucharist and ritual of re-commitment

Banquet honoring those who have anniversaries

FOLLOW-UP SECTION

V. KEEPING THE VISION BEFORE OUR EYES

A writing committee will take the proceedings, summarize them in a useful written form and distribute them.

The Priestly Life and Ministry Cluster will make plans on how to keep the vision before our eyes, build on it, and plan follow-up assemblies and celebrations.

VI. SHARING THE VISION

Collaborate with diocesan communications office on how to share this vision with the people of the diocese

CHAPTER 7
THE ROLES AND PROMISES OF CELIBACY AND OBEDIENCE FOR INTENTIONAL PRESBYTERATES

———— ഇ ————

THE ROLES AND PROMISES OF CELIBACY AND OBEDIENCE FOR INTENTIONAL PRESBYTERATES

The world doesn't want to hear about the labor pains.
It only wants to see the baby.
Johnny Sain

Diocesan priests do not take vows, but do make two important promises to the bishop: celibacy and obedience. Both, rather than being negatives, make complete availability for apostolic service possible.

1. Celibacy

Celibacy comes from the Latin (caelebs) meaning "single." Celibacy is the religious practice of devoting the time, love, energy and attention one would give a spouse and family over to the service of God's people. Celibacy makes complete availability for apostolic service possible. The celibate commitment has remained the most radical and comprehensive translation of Jesus' call to give up everything for the sake of the kingdom.

For many centuries, the Roman Catholic church has required that all its ordained ministers, with the exception of permanent deacons, live a celibate life-style. This long tradition, reaffirmed by Vatican Council II and subsequently by Popes

Paul VI and John Paul II, is the result of many centuries of reflection about the style of life appropriate to ordained ministry.

Celibacy is a heroic life-style for the healthy and well-adjusted person. Celibacy can actually be dangerous for the twisted, sexually repressed person. As we have learned so painfully recently, the damage unhealthy priests can do to the church is immeasurable. It takes a highly evolved spiritual person to freely and consciously embrace celibacy and do it justice. Most simply accept it and wrestle with it throughout their lives, sometimes carrying it like a cross, and living it one day at a time while relying on God's help each and every day.

There has been a lot of pious exaggeration written about celibacy. If it has any meaning at all in today's church, it is for the purpose of freeing one up for a greater good, for full-time service to God's people.

2. Obedience

Obedience, like celibacy, frees one up for complete availability to perform apostolic service. For the good of the church and its service to God's people, diocesan priests make a promise of obedience to their bishop and his successors. This promise has implications beyond the person of the bishop; it includes a promise to fellow members of a presbyterate. Rather than making one a slave to one particular person, it is really a promise to be "team player" with the bishop and the other members of the presbyterate, a promise to move from "my heart" to "our heart," as one priest put it.

An intentional presbyterate can only happen when individual priests not only make this promise of obedience, but also translate it into reality. It is really about promising to work as a team for the good of the people we serve. The promise of obedience may help even more than celibacy to make "intentional presbyterates" possible because, at its root, it is a promise to be a "team player" for the sake of our common purpose as diocesan priests.

CHAPTER 8
ADEQUATE
PRESBYTERATES:
A DIOCESAN
RESPONSIBILITY

—————— හ ——————

ADEQUATE PRESBYTERATES: A DIOCESAN RESPONSIBILITY

"Listen, Moses. You've got too many people reporting to you.
We're never going to get to the Promised Land if you don't
delegate some power!"
Jethro to Moses (paraphrased)

The task of fostering vocations to the diocesan priesthood is the responsibility of the whole Christian community.

- The whole Christian community does so by living in a fully Christian way

- Families do so by being alive with the spirit of faith and love and by suggesting diocesan priesthood to their sons as a possible vocation to consider

- Parishes do so by being communities in whose pulsating vitality young people themselves have a part

- Teachers and all others who, in any capacity, provide for the training of young men do so by helping them be able to recognize a divine calling and respond willingly to it

- Every priest does so by manifesting the zeal of an apostle in fostering vocations; by attracting the hearts of young men to the priesthood by their own humble lives, joyfully pursued; and by love for his fellow priests and brotherly collaboration with them.

- The bishop does so by seeing to it that all vocational resources and activities are closely coordinated and by helping those he judges to be called to the Lord's service

Such an active partnership should foster vocations to diocesan priesthood with discretion and zeal and should neglect no appropriate helps that modern psychology and sociology can offer.[46]

Even if all vocation directors were energetic, enthusiastic and talented, they could not, nor should they have to, do vocation ministry alone. In times when vocations flourished, there were few vocation offices and even fewer vocation personnel. Encouragement of vocations to priesthood was an ordinary part of church life. Today there is a need to involve, once again, every dimension of church life in encouraging and supporting vocations.

The church needs priests to further its work. As St. Ignatius of Antioch wrote, "Without bishops, presbyters and deacons, one cannot speak of the church." That conviction alone should move the whole church to action. "You will receive all that you pray for, provided you have faith." (Matthew 21:22) The "vocation crisis" in the church is possibly, at its root, a "crisis of faith." "The problem of faith today is especially that of unbelief among believers."[47]

CHAPTER 9
CONCLUSION

———— ℘ ————

CONCLUSION

If I were to wish for anything I should not wish for wealth and
power, but for the passionate sense of what can be, for the eyes,
which, ever young and ardent, see the possible.
Soren Kierkegaard

The catch phrase *downward spiraling talk* stands for a
resigned way of speaking that excludes possibility. Every industry or profession has its own version of downward spiraling talk, as does every relationship. Focusing on
the abstraction of scarcity, downward spiraling talk creates an
unassailable story about the limits to what is possible and tells
us compellingly how things are going from bad to worse. The
more attention you shine on a particular subject, the more
evidence of it will grow. Attention is like light and air and wa-
ter. Shine attention on obstacles and problems, and they multiply lavishly.[48]

On the other hand, *upward spiraling talk* can create a different reality. Shine attention on opportunities and possibilities, and they too will multiply lavishly. Things change dramatically when we care enough to seize what we love and give
it everything.

Often, the person in the group who articulates the possible
is rejected like a "prophet in his own country" or dismissed as
a dreamer by people who pride themselves on their supposed
realism. However, the fact of the matter is that we can do this
if we think we can. "Those who think they can and those who
think they can't are both right." (Henry Ford)

Intentional presbyterates, the corporate sense of priestly
identity and mission, although not fully developed even in official church documents, is clearly emerging as an important
direction for the future. It is still a goal, a dream.

Translating a dream into reality takes great courage. Doubt and laziness are constant enemies. When doubt and laziness reign, there is a strong temptation to let go of part of the dream as a way of resolving inevitable tensions. Success depends on the ability to remain enthusiastic, focused and purposeful to the end.

"For the vision still has its time, presses on to fulfillment, and will not disappoint; if it delays, wait for it, it will surely come, it will not be late."
HABBAKUK 2:3

"Behold, I make all things new."
REVELATION 21:5

I have set before you life and death, the blessing and the curse. Choose life, then, that you and your descendents may live, by loving the Lord, your God, heeding his voice, and holding fast to him. For that will mean life for you ..."
DEUTERONOMY 30:19,20

Keep watch over yourselves and over the flock the Holy Spirit has given you to guard.
ACTS 20:28

Do not neglect the gift you received when ... the presbyters laid their hands on you. Attend to your duties; let them absorb you, so that everyone may see your progress. Watch yourself and watch your teaching. Persevere in both tasks. By doing so you will bring to salvation yourself and all who hear you."
I TIMOTHY 4:14-16

Our deepest fear is not that we are inadequate. Our deepest fear is that we are powerful beyond measure. It is our light, not our darkness, that most frightens us. And as we let our light shine, we unconsciously give other people permission to do the same.
MARRIANNE WILLIAMSON

END NOTES

END NOTES

1. *Code of Canon Law,* Canon Law Society of America, Washington, DC, 1983, Canon 245, no. 2.

2. Abbott, Walter M., General Editor, and Joseph Gallagher, Translation Editor, "Decree on the Ministry and Life of Priests," *Documents of Vatican II,* New York, NY, 1966, Chapter II, nos. 2, 3.

3. *The Basic Plan for the Ongoing Formation of Priests,* United States Catholic Conference, Inc., Washington, DC, 2001, p. 93.

4. "Decree on the Ministry and Life of Priests," Chapter II, no. 8, and *Catechism of the Catholic Church,* Liguori Publications, Liguori, MO, 1994 translation, no. 1568.

5. Cf. Bibliography.

6. McQuaid, Rev. Tom, in a promotional brochure for Mundelein Seminary, Mundelein, IL.

7. Cozzens, Donald B., Ed., *The Spirituality of the Diocesan Priest,* The Liturgical Press, Collegeville, MN, 1997, p. 15 (Robert Schwartz).

8. "Decree on the Ministry and Life of Priests," Chapter II, no. 8.

9. "Decree on the Bishops' Pastoral Office in the Church," *Documents of Vatican II,* Chapter III, no. 34.

10. "Decree on the Ministry and Life of Priests," Chapter II, no. 8.

11. Ibid., footnotes no. 104, 105.

12. *As One Who Serves,* United States Catholic Conference, Washington, DC, 1977, p. 24.

13. "Dogmatic Constitution on the Church," *Documents of Vatican II,* Chapter III, no. 28, and "Decree on the Ministry and Life of Priests," Chapter II, nos. 7, 8.

14. *The Basic Plan for the Ongoing Formation of Priests,* p. 93.

15. Ibid., p. 93.

16. "Decree on the Ministry and Life of Priests," Chapter II, no. 8.

17. *The Basic Plan for the Ongoing Formation of Priests,* p. 94.

18. Ibid., p. 95.

19. Ibid., p. 95.

20. "Decree on the Ministry and Life of Priests," Chapter II, nos. 7, 11, and Chapter III, nos. 17, 21.

21. *The Basic Plan for the Ongoing Formation of Priests,* p. 98.

22. Cozzens, Donald B., *The Changing Face of the Priesthood,* The Liturgical Press, Collegeville, MN, 2000, pp. 47, 48.

23. *The Bridge Magazine,* Interview with Bishop Wilton Gregory, University of Saint Mary of the Lake/Mundelein Seminary, Mundelein, IL, Winter 2002/03, p. 3.

24. Aschenbrenner, George A., *Quickening the Fire in Our Midst,* Loyola Press, Chicago, IL, 2002, p. 133.

25. *The Basic Plan for the Ongoing Formation of Priests,* p. 93.

26. Levoy, Gregg, *Callings: Finding and Following an Authentic Life,* Three Rivers Press, New York, NY, 1997, p. 316.

27. *Directory for the Life and Ministry of Priests,* Libreria Editrice Vaticana, Città del Vaticano, 1994, no. 25.

28. Kicanas, Gerald F., "The Heart and Core of Diocesan Priesthood," *Vocation Journal,* National Conference of Diocesan Vocation Directors, Little River, SC, 2002, Vol. 4, p. 49.

29. "Decree on Priestly Formation," *Documents of Vatican II,* Chapter II, No. 2.

30. Peck, M. Scott, *The Road Less Traveled,* Simon & Schuster, Inc., New York, NY, 1978, pp. 45-46.

31. Ibid., pp. 276-277.

32. *Directory for the Life and Ministry of Priests,* No. 27.

33. Drummond, Thomas B., "Sexual Misbehavior and the Infused Competency Myth," *The New Life Institute for Human Development Newsletter,* The New Life Institute, Middleburg, VA, Winter 2003, Vol. 11, No. 1.

34. Hoge, Dean R., *The First Five Years of the Priesthood,* The Liturgical Press, Collegeville, MN, 2002, p. 101.

35. *The Basic Plan for the Ongoing Formation of Priests,* pp. 95-98.

36. *The Priest and the Third Christian Millennium,* United States Catholic Conference, Washington, DC, 1999, Chapter 4, no. 3.

37. *Origins,* United States Conference of Catholic Bishops, Washington, DC, Vol. 18, no. 31, Jan. 12, 1989.

38. Pope John Paul II, *I Will Give You Shepherds,* St. Paul Books & Media, Boston, MA, 1992, no. 76.

39. Howe, Neil, and William Strauss, *Millennials Rising: The Next Great Generation,* Vintage Books, New York, NY, 2000, pp. 3-29.

40. "Decree on the Bishops' Pastoral Office in the Church," Chapter II, no. 16.

41. *The Basic Plan for the Ongoing Formation of Priests,* p. 97.

42. Quinn, Bernard, Ed., "Ecumenical Planning for Mission" in *Town and Country,* CARA, Washington, DC, 1968, p. 74.

43. Pope John Paul II, *I Will Give You Shepherds,* no. 79.

44. de Becker, Paul, "A Priest Alone," *The Tablet,* London, Great Britain, April 27, 1996, p. 540.

45. Kicanas, Gerald F., *"Three Goals for Vocations Directors: Priesthood,"* United States Conference for Catholic Bishops, <http://www.nccbuscc.org/vocations/articles/kicanas.htm>(July 11, 2003), p. 7.

46. "Decree on Priestly Formation," Chapter II, no. 2.

47. Rolheiser, Ronald, *The Shattered Lantern: Rediscovering a Felt Presence of God,* The Crossroad Publishing Company, New York, NY, 2001, p. 17.

48. Zander, Rosemund Stone, and Benjamin Zander, *The Art of Possibility,* Harvard Business School Press, Boston, MA, 2000, p. 108.

BIBLIOGRAPHY

BIBLIOGRAPHY

As One Who Serves, United States Catholic Conference, Washington, DC, 1977.

Aschenbrenner, George A., *Quickening the Fire in Our Midst,* Loyola Press, Chicago, IL, 2002.

The Bridge Magazine, "Interview with Bishop Wilton Gregory," University of Saint Mary of the Lake/Mundelein Seminary, Mundelein, IL, Winter 2002/03.

Abbott, Walter M., General Editor, and Joseph Gallagher, Translation Editor, *The Documents of Vatican II,* Guild Press, New York, NY, 1966.

The Basic Plan for the Ongoing Formation of Priests, United States Catholic Conference, Inc., Washington, DC, 2001.

Catechism of the Catholic Church, Liguori Publications, Liguori, MO, 1994 Translation.

Code of Canon Law, Canon 245, No. 2, Canon Law Society of America, Washington, DC, 1983.

Cozzens, Donald B., *The Changing Face of the Priesthood,* The Liturgical Press, Collegeville, MN, 2000.

Cozzens, Donald B., Ed., *The Spirituality of the Diocesan Priest,* The Liturgical Press, Collegeville, MN, 1997.

de Becker, Paul, "A Priest Alone," *The Tablet,* London, Great Britain, April 27, 1996.

Directory for the Life and Ministry of Priests, Libreria Editrice Vaticana, Città del Vaticano, 1994.

Drummond, Thomas B., "Sexual Misbehavior and the Infused Competency Myth," *The New Life Institute for Human Development Newsletter,* The New Life Institute, Middleburg, VA, Winter 2003, Vol. 11, No. 1.

Hoge, Dean R., *The First Five Years of the Priesthood,* The Liturgical Press, Collegeville, MN, 2002.

Howe, Neil, and William Strauss, *Millennials Rising: The Next Great Generation,* Vintage Books, New York, NY, 2000.

Kicanas, Gerald F., "The Heart and Core of Diocesan Priesthood," *Vocation Journal,* National Conference of Diocesan Vocation Directors, Little River, SC, Vol. 4, p. 49, 2002.

Kicanas, Gerald F., *"Three Goals for Vocations Directors: Priesthood,"* United States Conference for Catholic Bishops, <http://www.nccbuscc.org/vocations/articles/kicanas.htm> (July 11, 2003).

Levoy, Gregg, *Callings: Finding and Following an Authentic Life,* Three Rivers Press, New York, NY, 1997.

Peck, M. Scott, *The Road Less Traveled,* Simon & Schuster, Inc., New York, NY, 1978.

Pope John Paul II, *I Will Give You Shepherds,* St. Paul Books & Media, Boston, MA, 1992.

The Priest and the Third Christian Millennium, United States Catholic Conference, Washington, DC, 1999.

Quinn, Bernard, Ed., "Ecumenical Planning for Mission" in *Town and Country,* CARA, Washington, DC, 1968.

Rolheiser, Ronald, *The Shattered Lantern: Rediscovering a Felt Presence of God,* The Crossroad Publishing Company, New York, NY, 2001.

U.S. Bishops' Committee on Vocations, *The National Strategy: "A Future Full of Hope," A Natural Plan for Vocations,* United States Conference for Catholic Bishops, Secretariat for Vocations and Priestly Formation, Washington, DC, June 2003.

Zander, Rosemund Stone, and Benjamin Zander, *The Art of Possibility,* Harvard Business School Press, Boston, MA, 2000.